Pharmaceutical Sales
Exposed!

THE INSIDER SECRETS THEY DON'T
WANT YOU TO KNOW ABOUT

By Sterling Wolfgang

Table of Contents

An Important Message

After a considerable amount of thought as to whether or not I should write this tell all book. I decided that I must reveal this valuable information for the countless number of people who deserve to know the true intentions the pharmaceutical industry has for the public and especially those individuals who want to work or who are currently working in pharmaceutical sales.

As a matter fact, it concerns me deeply when I see all of the TV commercials everyday promoting all of the countless numbers of brand name medications each and every day. It upsets me deeply. I just cannot stand by allowing so many uninformed ,hopeful individuals without this knowledge to be taken advantage of by companies that are only wanting to use them as life-long highly medicated zombies who are hooked on their drugs.

And so far as those people who are considering a job in this industry as well as those people who are already working in pharmaceutical sales. I truly feel that to have to begin a career in this industry these days without this knowledge. The individual who does is doomed to encounter many , many very difficult and sometimes painful challenges and decisions that could very easily change their life in negative way forever. As well as encountering possible multi-million dollar fines and possible imprisonment for the sales representative who is not aware of the true situation he or she is getting into. While on the other hand if a person starts their new career off with this wisdom and knowledge. That person will be safeguarded from most of the virtual landmines that await you.

So it is my hope that by writing this book the reader of this book will have all of the information he or she needs in order to make a well informed decision of whether or not you should allow yourself to become a lifelong customer of any pharmaceutical company and instead find alternative ways to get the medical help you need without becoming a pharmaceutical industry zombie. And for the person who to accepts a job in pharmaceutical sales you will be very well informed. Because without a doubt there are a number of things your new boss and employer will not tell you in the beginning and only after time spent on the job will these things begin to reveal themselves to you. Now you won't have to spend over 35 years along with a lot of pain and suffering to find out the truth.

I have found this to be the case many times over the years and I just don't think that is the way business should be done. So I urge you to take the time to read this book well and go forth in your quest with the knowledge and wisdom I am sure you will need. Additionally, I think that in order to survive in this business as a pharmaceutical sales representative today you have to develop a different mindset about what this job truly has to offer you.

You must remember that this job no longer offers a lifetime of employment security where you will work for the same company for 30-40 years. Those days are gone forever. As a matter of fact, if you should decide to maintain a career in this industry you will probably end of working for 6-8 different pharmaceutical companies over a 10-20 year period of time. These days pharmaceutical sales provides an excellent opportunity to learn advanced sales skills and management skills that you can then use later on in your life within some other occupation or entrepreneurial enterprise. But you must not ever think of the job as a permanent solution to your longer term financial needs. Because I can promise you that you will be disappointed. These days and for many years to come pharmaceutical sales will only offer you many temporary employment opportunities. That is if you can meet the industries new standards of requirements for the people they select. So, one piece of wisdom that I can share with you that I know will best prepare you for your future in pharmaceutical sales should decide to maintain a career in this industry is to, **Expect The Unexpected and You Will Never Be Surprised!**

Chapter 1

In The Beginning There Was Big Pharma

Over 35 years ago I began my career in pharmaceutical sales. That was probably one of the happiest days of my life. Because for many years prior to entering pharmaceutical sales I had heard of what a wonderful career it was. And truthfully so. Over 35 years ago a person could go to work for a pharmaceutical company and be assured they would have a job until they retired. As a matter of fact there were a few people who I met over the years who had already been in pharmaceutical sales for at least 40 years. And based on the cloths they wore, the cars they drove and the homes they lived in. It was very, very clear they were making at least $120K or more a year. As I began to learn more and more about these people I could hardly believe the lifestyles they were living.

They worked from home, set their own schedules each day, drove a company car, entertained the doctors at the most expensive restaurants in town, played golf a couple of times a week and traveled to 5 star resorts around the world. As a result of getting to know these people it was very easy for me to decide this was what I wanted to do for a living for the rest of my life.

So after trying very hard for several years I managed to secure a job in pharmaceutical sales with a major pharmaceutical company. And just as I had imagined it was great!

I would never have imagined that over my 35 year career I would end up working for 3 of the top contract sales organizations, working on at least 11 different contracts, working for 7 different major pharmaceutical companies, launched 5 different major drugs and sold over 20 different pharmaceutical products during my career. And I have been laid off so many times that it is hard to even count the variations in the different reasons the companies gave for laying off the sales force. Wow what a crazy mixed up ride it has been!

However since early 1990 the industry has drastically changed. A person who worked in pharmaceutical sales 10, 15 as far back as 35 years ago definitely made an above average income and was secure in knowing the company would not just dump them into the unemployment lines just in order to increase the company's bottom line. I can promise you today is a new day. Pharmaceutical companies today do not think twice about laying off hundreds of thousands of people at the drop of a hat.

In the early years pharmaceutical sales represented The Perfect Employment Opportunity. Because if you managed to get hired by a major pharmaceutical company. You could rest assured they were going to take you in and basically make you apart of the family for life. Usually after you were hires a standard process began. You would receive a very nice welcome letter from the president of the company or one of the upper level management people. In some cases you might even receive a personal phone call from one of the big boys themselves.

Then within a day or so you would receive a special package by mail strategically explaining all of the requirements you would need to fulfill as a part of the educational training process. Then within another day or so you would receive a big box full of books for you to begin studying in order to learn the new product or products you will soon be selling. Usually this home-study process lasted about 2 weeks. After which time you will then be sent to a special training center to complete your product training. As well as to enable you to take the required product tests in order to become certified that you are qualified to go out into the field to sell the product or products you would be responsible for.

Also somewhere along the way you would have been given the option to select a company car from a list of cars offered by the company. Then after this initial process is when all of the real fun would begin because now you would be able to go out into the new territory and begin interacting with the medical community.

In the early days pharmaceutical sales representatives were very well respected members of the medical community. Doctors ,nurses and pharmacists actually looked forward to seeing the pharmaceutical representative coming into the offices and pharmacies in order to provide them with important medical information. As well as having the representative spend quality time with them in order to get to know each other and learn as much as possible about the company's product or products. However now technology has changed the industry forever, As a matter of fact, already more and more companies are investing in a fairly new technology process called e-detailing that allows a doctor to decide when her or she wants to be detailed online via a completely electronic process by a recorded product presentation or by a virtual sales rep presentation. As a result there will soon be fewer and fewer jobs available for the traditional pharmaceutical sales representative. By utilizing this new technology pharmaceutical companies will save multi millions of dollars every years since they will not have to incur all of the expenses of hiring , managing and maintaining a large field force.

In the early days of pharmaceutical sales companies allowed their representatives to spend as much quality time as needed in order to build rapport, get to know all of the office staff and to thoroughly educate the doctor and the entire staff on the benefits of the company's products. But not any more. Things have really changed.

Chapter 2

The Dream Begins To Unravel

Now the focus of the majority of the major pharmaceutical companies has changed. These days he majority of the pharmaceutical representatives find themselves caught in a high pressured situation to simply get signatures from doctors, drop off samples and try to give a quick 20-40 second sales presentation to 8-10 very busy doctors a day. In addition to driving as far as 2 hours from home each day in order to get to the territory they will be working in for the day. In the earlier days that was unheard of. That would have been considered too much windshield time.

Now don't get me wrong there are some days a representative will be able to work closer to home. But for the most part the majority of the territory is as far away as at least 2 hours away. Which means the representative will travel at least 1000-2000 miles every month.

Then in addition to all that the majority of pharmaceutical companies have created a territory management system which requires the already stressed out pharmaceutical sales representative to make sales calls on at least 100-150 key doctors in the territory 1-2 times within a 3-4 month period of time. No matter where that doctor might be located in the territory.

So if you take all of this into consideration here is how it all works these days. This is important for you to know especially if you are still considering whether or not you want to get into this business.

A Real World Day In The Life of A Pharmaceutical Sales Representative

Based on the size of the territory the pharmaceutical sales representative is required to leave home between the hours of 7am-8am. Keep in mind the job description will say that you should work from 8am-5pm daily. But the reality of the matter is after you except the responsibility for the territory. You will have to decide just how early you will need to get up each morning in order to be able to drive to the part of the territory you will be working in that day. So if you have a 2 hour drive to get to your territory. And you want to arrive at your first doctor's office by 9:00am. Then you will have to leave home around 7:00am.

So, say for an example that you will have to leave home at 7:00am. You pack the car the night before with all of the appropriate sales literature you will need and all the product samples you will need for the day. You are also required to do what is called pre-call planning for each of the 8-10 doctors you hope to see the next day. But you really need to plan to see more than 8-10 doctors because there is a very high chance that at least 2-3 of the doctors you plan to see won't be able to see you.

By the way if you don't already know it. Your pre-call planning is done based on several criteria that you must research on each of the doctors you plan to see. Which usually involves knowing what products the doctor is currently prescribing ,what insurance plans the doctor utilizes as well as what message you want to deliver in order to sell your product. All of this advanced preparation must be done before you ever step foot in front of the doctors you plan to see each day. After all of this pre-calling planning work has been done then you are ready to go to work.

The next day comes and you are ready to leave home and travel to your territory. You get up bright and early to leave home. You drive 2 hours to the city you will be working in. You arrive at the doctor's office and as you had planned you are right on time. The only problem is that when you arrive there are already 3 or 4 other pharmaceutical sales representatives there ahead of you waiting to see the same doctor. Sometimes even more than that. Sometimes there is a small crowd of pharmaceutical sales reps waiting to see the same doctor.

So you do what any good pharmaceutical sales representative would do and you decide to wait your turn.

After all this particular doctor is a very, very good customer of yours and you really need to see him in order to sell your product and to meet your company's requirement of seeing him a 1-2 times sometimes more with a 3-4 month period of time. The question now becomes how long do you wait? If you are like most good pharmaceutical sales representatives you will wait anywhere from 1-2 hours to get to see this important doctor. Why would you wait this long you might ask? Well there are many very good reasons you would possibly wait that long. The first good reason you would possibly wait that long is because as I said earlier this is one of your most important doctors. He is one of your best customers. And if your want him to continue being one of your best customers you have to continue to remind him of all the reasons he is prescribing your products. As well as to leave him or her lots of samples of your product. You see many doctors have a policy of prescribing only those products in which they have samples of. If you don't see him then you will not be in a position to leave him any of your samples.

You see along with everything I have already mentioned which is a requirement of the job itself.

In order to stay in good standings and keep your job. A pharmaceutical sales representative is also required to achieve and maintain a 60%-90% sampling quota. The representative must also achieve a 60%-90% quota of how many times the representative must stand face to face with the doctor and make a sales presentation. The representative must also meet a quota of seeing each of the 100-150 key targeted doctors in the territory 1-3 maybe 6 times within a 3-4 month period of time.

Then there are the required sales quotas that are set for the pharmaceutical sales representative. These must also be taken into consideration when doing the jobs because after all if a representative cannot bring in the right amount of sales that representative will eventually be replaced. In most cases they will give the under performing representative an opportunity to increase his or her sales.

Chapter 3

The Beginning of The End

In 1991 when the politicians in Washington began talking about healthcare reform it was as if the pharmaceutical industry was about to have a nervous breakdown. As soon as the news hit the streets that the government was considering making some major changes in the healthcare industry. Pharmaceutical companies immediately began maneuvering themselves and repositioning themselves in order to be able to survive and protect their multi-billion dollar empires.

Never before had I seen so many pharmaceutical companies begin to pushing some people to retire. As well as beginning a process of downsizing , reorganizing and laying off workers around the world. For the first time in over at least 50 years had the pharmaceutical industry began to layoff its sales people during a time when the economy was still doing alright. And believe me prior to this you would have never heard of a pharmaceutical company laying off its sales force. That was unheard of . But this was really just the beginning of what was to come in the near future.

Because it seems that once this process began it turned into a major epidemic of layoffs and mergers of many different pharmaceutical companies. And many people learned whenever 2 pharmaceutical companies merge through a buyout.

That normally means that there will be a major layoff. And you never know how that is going to play out. Sometimes people from the buying company get laid off , sometimes people from the company that was bought get laid off and sometimes a few hundred people from both companies get laid off. You just never know.

It seems as if from the layoffs from the early 1990s the pharmaceutical industry realized that it could begin eliminating millions of dollars in expenses and people that was acquired over the prior 50-60 years before. Now they had found a way to just get rid of the debt by simply getting rid of thousands of people. Mainly the pharmaceutical sales representatives. As a result of studying the pharmaceutical industry for over 30 years I have found that whenever the economy get tough or whenever the industry is going through some kind of tough times or changes begin to occur. One of the first things they will do is layoff thousands of sales people.

Then came the Big Lawsuits! This has been another major blow to the pharmaceutical industry. It seems that over the years more and more people have begun to seek legal counsel as a result of a number of different adverse reactions or death due to a pharmaceutical product. As a result the legal profession has recognized and targeted the pharmaceutical industry as a major cash cow. And as a result the pharmaceutical industry represented a brand new Multi Billion Dollar potential ocean of money to be collected on. All they have to do is find the people who have had these problems. Low and behold!! We all began to see lots and lots of television commercials and full page ads looking for those individuals who need legal counsel as a result of a problem pharmaceutical product. As a result this cost the pharmaceutical companies Billions of Dollars. And as a result what have they done. They have begun to layoff thousands and thousands of pharmaceutical sales representative.

As a matter of fact over the horizon for the pharmaceutical industry is another major shakeup. You see due to the fact that most of the major pharmaceutical companies have product pipelines that are drying up or they have major products that will soon be going generic. Many very large pharmaceutical companies will soon begin to lose Billions of Dollars in profits. And what do you think will begin to happen when this time comes. Well 2 things are going to happen. First you will see an epidemic of mergers and buyout between pharmaceutical companies and you will see another epidemic of drastic field force layoffs.

Do you see a trend here? Well just in case you don't. Every time the pharmaceutical industry goes through some kind of potential threat on the industry or these days when ever they feel like it they lay off more pharmaceutical representatives. Over the last 20 years I have seen this happen over and over again starting about 1991. And it is continuing to happen over and over again. All you have to do is watch the new daily. If you do it enough you will get good enough to begin seeing the writing on the wall. And you too will be able to accurately predict the next wave of layoffs before the happen. But that's not all. Because the layoffs have only just begun. There are many more layoffs to come. You see from all my research the industry is really going to through a major paradigm shift from carrying the total expenses of each maintaining full time field forces to simply contracting this expense out to Contract Pharmaceutical Companies otherwise known as Contract Sales Organization or CSOs.

Actually instead of calling it Contract Pharmaceutical Sales it should be called Temporary Pharmaceutical Sales. Because the name contract pharmaceutical sales is very misleading. That name makes the representative feel as if there is some degree of security about the job. When in fact there is no security in contract pharmaceutical sales at all.

Important Note

Always remember that in contract pharmaceutical sales, anything can happen! Your job can just disappear overnight.

Chapter 4

The Truth About Contract Pharmaceutical Sales

In an earlier chapter I talked about how in 1991 major pharmaceutical companies began downsizing and laying off thousands of its sales people. Well I am sorry to say this process is just beginning because during the ongoing evolution of the pharmaceutical industry another phenomenon is now taking place. As I briefly mentioned in the last chapter a somewhat new industry is gaining popularity over the last 10-12 years. This somewhat new industry is called Contract Pharmaceutical Sales. Otherwise known as the Contract Sales Organization. While this new organizational structure is not totally new. It's popularity and use by major pharmaceutical companies has gained significant momentum and will continue until pharmaceutical sales as we know it today no longer exists.

You see Big Pharma otherwise known as the major pharmaceutical companies has realized that by utilizing a Contract Sales Organization it can all but eliminate one of the most costly expenses associated with marketing a pharmaceutical product. That is the field sales force. By contracting this aspect of marketing a pharmaceutical product now all the manufacturing pharmaceutical company has to do is to do what it does best. That is doing the research and development of the pharmaceutical product or products. Without any of the expenses of paying for and maintaining a dedicated field sales force.

What this means to the manufacturing pharmaceutical company is now the company does not have to pay for all the many expenses associated with managing a dedicated sales force such as salaries ,insurance benefits, company cars and all the other expenses that comes with having permanent sales people. Instead by using a Contract Sales Organization the Contract Sales Company is now responsible for all these expenses. Even better yet. Whenever the big pharmaceutical company feels that it no longer needs this Temporary Field Force. All it has to do is push a button or make a phone call to get the process started for ending the business relationship. It's just that easy because when the initial contract is being developed the client or the manufacturing pharmaceutical company includes in the contract an escape clause that enables the company to get out of the deal without any or very little financial loss. In most cases all the client or the manufacturing pharmaceutical company has to do is give a 30,60 or 90 day notice to the Contract Pharmaceutical Company. In some cases they only have to give a 2 week notice. The problem is you will never know which kind of escape clause was written into the contract. So what that means to the contract pharmaceutical sales representative is the representative never knows from one month to the next whether or not he or she will have a job. So almost overnight the lives of hundreds of people and sometimes thousands of people are turned upside down. All in part because the sales people were led to believe they had a contract which would last for 1,2, 3 or whatever length of time they were told. The truth of the matter is the not anyone on the Contract Pharmaceutical Sales side of the deal who really knows with absolute certainty how long a pharmaceutical sales contract will last.

The extreme downside for the contract pharmaceutical sales person is he or she does not have enough time to begin preparing for the prospect of losing their primary source of income.

What's so sad is that over the years I have seen some very sad situations where both the husband and the wife have been laid off at the same time from 2 different contract pharmaceutical companies. I have also seen just as many single people who laid off basically lose everything they own because they could not find another job in the same salary range as they had when they sold pharmaceutical sales. When this happens families are all but destroyed. It would seem that contract pharmaceutical sales companies would have a better system in place to make sure that when one contract ends.

The people who are losing their jobs should be soon placed on another contract within a reasonable length of time or these people are kept on salary until they are placed on another contract by the contract company. It is also sad that when a contract ends no matter how it ends the people who lose their jobs have to wait to be interviewed by a new hiring manager. In other words their resume is thrown back into the pile of resume with all the other thousands of candidates.

Then if they are lucky enough to have their resume selected then they will get a chance to interview. And they will have to begin the interviewing process just as if they were a totally new candidate from outside the company. They say they give preference to a person with a prior work history with the company but I know they don't always do it.

To make matters worse Contract Pharmaceutical Sales is the wave of the future in the pharmaceutical sales industry. Because as I said earlier for the first time in many decades the pharmaceutical industry has identified a way for it to stay very profitable in an ever changing healthcare marketplace. Already more and more pharmaceutical companies have already begun to layoff their permanent sales forces in order to begin utilizing contract pharmaceutical organization. If you watch the news every few weeks you hear or read about another major pharmaceutical laying off their permanent sales people. Then if you listen closely you will find that the same company will turn around and contract those same positions out to a Contract Pharmaceutical Sales Company. Not to mention that many times some of the new people that are hired to do the job are hired at a significant reduced salary. As a matter of fact I have know some pharmaceutical sales people to be laid off by the manufacturing company and then be rehired as a contract sales person at a lower salary for doing the same job. What a shame.

Important Note

Always remember that in contract pharmaceutical sales, anything can happen! Your job can vanish overnight.

Chapter 5

Never Believe a Word They Say

Here is another subject that big pharmaceutical companies and contract pharmaceutical companies don't want to know about. You see due to the fact that contract pharmaceutical companies are under so much pressure to produce the agreed upon sales goals. They will say almost anything they feel will keep their sales people in place and in the field.

Here are several of the things you should listen for so you will know when you are being misled by your manager or upper management:

1. If you do a really good job selling this product the client is probably going to hire as permanent employees the most successful sales people on this contract. If you do a good job that could be you. They sometimes call this rolling over to work for the client. **Not Completely True** (Because these days and in the future the trend is not for major drug companies to hire new permanent sales people. Instead they want to use contract sales people. Also if you go to work for the client pharmaceutical sales company. If you get laid off you are totally out on your own looking for a job.)

2. I am sure this contract will continue for the duration of the contract. **Not True** (No manager can honestly say that. Nobody knows except the client.)

3. If you do a good job on this contract I will personally help you and hire you on my new team once I find a new contract. **Not Completely True** (Because managers are just as vulnerable as sales representatives are when it comes to losing their jobs. When a contract ends they are just like everyone else racing around like rats trying to find a new job. So they might not be able to help you because they might not even have a job themselves. It's not uncommon for a person who was a sales manager on one contract to end up as a sales person on a new contract. So a person who was once your manager could very easily be your sales partner on a new contract. Or visa versa. So be careful who you tell all you personal secrets too.)

4. Even though our salary is lower you will make it up in bonus commissions. **Not True.** (Nobody can accurately predict how much commission a sale person will make on a contract. It's a fact that contract pharmaceutical sales companies pay much lower salaries then Big Pharma. So don't let a hiring manager pull that line on you.)

5. Another message you should not buy into is when then say, The Client Is Really Happy With The Work We Are Doing On This Contract. **Don't**

believe it. (That message is just a ploy to make you feel comfortable that the contract is stable. It designed to make you feel comfortable so you won't start looking for another job. Remember they don't want you to leave the contract. It's just designed to keep you on the job. I've heard that message on several different contracts and then a week or so later the sales team is notified that contract has been canceled by the client.)

6. We like people who stay on the contract until the end. Or we really look out for people who stay on the contract until the end. **Not True** (When the contract ends your resume is thrown back into the pile with everyone else. Including those people from outside the company. Additionally the company you are working for has no hesitation to lay you off at any time before the contact ends. So why should you worry about them?)

7. If you happen to lose your job. **And this applies mainly to contract pharmaceutical sales.** I have found that when you are being notified that you are going to lose your job. The contract pharmaceutical company likes to give you some hope that everything is going to be OK by telling you that they have several new contract jobs that will soon be coming available. And that you will have an opportunity to apply for these new job opportunities. Well it has been my experience that

these jobs really never become a reality. Sometimes they do and sometimes they don't. But for the moment when you are being laid off of your job, it makes you feel better for a moment. I have said all of this to say. **Not Completely True** (Additionally the best thing for you to do is hope that it is true and if it is all well and good. But you should begin right away looking for a new job just in case the company does not have a job for you anytime soon.)

These are just a few of the most popular messages that are used to gain the confidence of the sales people in order to keep them on the jobs. Because these messages are only designed to make you feel as if your job is safe and you don't have anything to worry about. My advice to you is to always look out for yourself and your family. I can tell you that you are much better off with a permanent position inside the pharmaceutical company corporate offices or inside the contract pharmaceutical sales company corporate offices **but not in field sales**. **Field sales has become far too unpredictable.** Unless field sales is perfect for the lifestyle you want to live. Or if field sales allows you to set the stage for some other venture that you are working on. I suggest that you use the field sales job to work your way inside the corporate office in order to find a safe long term job opportunity. From the moment that you accept a position in contract pharmaceutical sales you should begin right away to put your feelers out looking for a more stable job within the corporation . If not within the corporation then you should begin to consider gaining some kind of special training for your new a new career while you are working on the contract. But don't make the mistake I have made and so many others by staying contract pharmaceutical sale. **Get out while you can!**

Important Note

Always remember that in contract pharmaceutical sales, anything can happen! Your job description can change overnight.

Here Are Several Very Important Indicators That You Are About To Get Laid Off

1. 1.If you begin hearing that different key people in upper management are leaving the company or accepting new jobs outside of the company. This especially applies if you are working in contract pharmaceutical sales.

2. If you begin to hear that more and more sales people are leaving the company. This especially applies if you are working in contract pharmaceutical sales.

3. If your manager starts having a lot of Family Emergencies and must take off work. Or if your manager starts taking a lot of vacation days. If anything your manager is interviewing for a new job. Or if your manager abruptly takes a new job.

4. If you notice that all normal communications from your manager or the company comes to a complete stop for a week or more. Something big is happening and most times it's not good for the sales people. This especially applies if you are working in contract pharmaceutical sales.

5. If you get an email, text message or a phone call instructing you there will be a mandatory teleconference that day, the next day or some day in the near future. This is not good. Especially if you are in contract pharmaceutical sales. This probably means you are going to be notified your job or the contract is coming to an end. On the teleconference they will tell you how much they appreciate all of your efforts but the company has decided to go into a different direct and your services will no longer be needed.

Important Note

Always remember that in contract pharmaceutical sales, anything can happen! Your territory can change overnight. And you might not even know it for weeks.

Chapter 6

Swimming With The Sharks On Steroids

These days working as a pharmaceutical sales representative is serious business. No longer can a sales representative venture out into the territory without the complete understanding that just as a doctor is held responsible and liable for the prescriptions he or she writes. So is the pharmaceutical sales representative held liable and responsible for the messages the representative communicates to the medical professional. The punishment for communicating the wrong message or an off label message to the medical professional can have serious legal and financial repercussions for the pharmaceutical sales representative valued at well over $50,000 or more. As well as possible imprisonment for the pharmaceutical sales representative. Which means that the things you say during the course of a routine day could change your life forever in ways you could never have imagined.

So it's sad to say that everyday thousands of unknowing pharmaceutical sales representatives venture out into their territories without stopping to think or realize just how serious a job they are really doing. As a result I want to stress the point that selling pharmaceuticals is **Serious business**.

And to make matters worse I have found that most contract pharmaceutical sales companies do not do a thorough enough job educating and stressing the seriousness of this situation with the new sales representatives as they go through training. Yes there is a very basic training program in place. But it does not do a complete enough job emphasizing all of the possible problem areas a sales representative can find themselves in. Thereby leaving the new pharmaceutical sales representative exposed to all kinds of possible legal and financial troubles that could all but destroy the life of an individual who does not have the financial means to hire the kind of attorneys required to try such a costly case. The other problem I have with the way most companies handle this subject with a new person who is interviewing for the job and who eventually ends up going to work for the company. There is no mention of this possible legal adversity until after the new hire has accepted the job and is well into the training process. In many cases there is not much emphasis on this subject until the last phase of the training process and the new hire as already committed themselves to the job.

So what I have done in an effort to give anyone who is considering a job in pharmaceutical sales. Or anyone who is already in pharmaceutical sales and has not seen the information. I have included with this report a copy of the actual document which is called the Prescription Drug Marketing Act of 1987. Please take the time to read over this government document very well so that you clearly understand the seriousness of the job you do or will soon be doing. The best way to describe what this business has become is it's just like Swimming With The Sharks On Steroids. **Because these days drug representatives are watching other drug representatives for off label marketing practices You have doctors who are trying to lure drug sales representatives into off label communications . And you have the media watching everyone for an opportunity to make some of the Big Money now available for catching a pharmaceutical sales representative in the act of doing something illegal. Everyone wants to make some of that easy money. It really is like** Swimming With The Sharks On Steroids. Also be sure to do a search online for any new updates or additions to this same document. Simply do a keyword search for The Prescription Drug Marketing Act. Be sure to read the copy I have given you here in the report. But be sure to periodically research the internet for a newer version on this document because the rules are always changing.

WARNING

THE PRESCRIPTION DRUG MARKETING ACT

If you take the time to read this government document you should be able to see that selling pharmaceutical sales **Is Serious Business** and should be done to the letter of the law. So if someone ever asks you to give them a few of your samples or a family member asks you for a few of your samples. Or if anyone ever suggests that you should sell them. **Don't Do It!!**

You must be aware of the fact that due to the rules of the game stated in the Prescription Drug Marketing Act. There are now lots of people in the marketplace watching your every move, every day. For instance there is a major financial reward for any representative who identifies another representative breaking any of these rules and there is also a major financial reward for any doctor who identifies a pharmaceutical sales representative who is illegally marketing a pharmaceutical product by selling the product off label or in some way other than what has been approved by the FDA.

Chapter 7

Landmines Are Everywhere

These days you really do have to watch very carefully where you step because there any many different virtual landmines that if stepped on during the course of doing the job of a pharmaceutical sales representative you could literally be blown away in the court of law. A few of the landmines I am referring to would be activities like the one mentioned in the prior chapter. Others would be off label marketing of a product. Another would be lack of the appropriate sample accountability, another would be misuse of expense funds. Another example would be recording inappropriate notes in your computer about a conversation with a customer, misuse of the company car, low sales call count, not reaching the sales goal, starting to work late, ending the day early etc, etc. The landmines are everywhere.

Here is a small list of actual criminal cases where different pharmaceutical sales representatives , district managers and their companies were charged by the government for various activities resulting from the illegal marketing of pharmaceutical products.

You should know and be very well aware of the fact that just because you work for a particular pharmaceutical company. That does not mean if you should find yourself in the middle of a legal battle resulting from your work as a pharmaceutical sales representative. The company you work for might or might not provide you with legal representation. Or support you financially in the criminal trial. Depending on what was involved you could find yourself responsible for a very expensive legal bill.

Over the years I have seen criminal cases of this nature where the company decided it was not in their best interest to financially support the representative and you know what that means.

1. **Pfizer-$2.3billion penalty**

2. **AstraZeneca-$355 million penalty**

3. **Abbott-$622 million penalty**

4. **Aventis-$190 million penalty**

5. **Bayer-$14 million penalty**

6. **Bayer-$257million penalty**

7. **Bristol-Myers Squibb-$515 million penalty**

8. **GSK-$87.6 million penalty**

9. **Genentech-$50 million penalty**

10. **Eli Lilly-$1.4 billion penalty**

11. **Tap Pharmaceutical Co-$875 million penalty**

12. **Pfizer-$430 million penalty**

13. **Schering-Plough-$435 million penalty**

14. **Merck & Co, Inc.-$650 million penalty**

15. **Eli Lilly and Company-$1.4 billion penalty**

Keep in mind these are not all of the cases on record involving pharmaceutical sales representatives who have been charged and prosecuted for doing something wrong on the job. There are just as many or more involving the misuse , injury or death of the user of the product. In some cases a sales representative as been involved in the case because of what the representative communicated to the doctor. If you want to find out more about any of the other legal cases involving pharmaceutical sales representatives you will need to go online and do a little research of your own.

Also keep in mind that whenever a pharmaceutical company has to pay these huge legal fees and penalties , that company is going to have to begin looking for ways to reduce their expenses. And as the trend has always proven. The company will eventually begin laying off it's employees. Especially the sales people.

Chapter 8

Pharmaceutical Sales Has Become A Real Rat Race

Now in this chapter we will take a look at 3 other very important variables which will significantly affect how difficult or how easy a representative is able to achieve all of these goals:

1. Time
2. Geography
3. Availablity

Let's first take a look at the **Time factor**. There is are only 8 working hours in a day in which a representative has to do the job. But actually a representative really has less than 8 hours a day in which to see doctors because most doctors offices close from 12:00 noon until 2:00pm. There are few that open back up at 1:00pm but most don't. So that being the situation a pharmaceutical sales representative only has 6 -7 hours a day to work. Maybe even less if you factor in travel times and the time a representative spends waiting to see each doctor. We must also factor in the fact that some doctors do not even begin seeing pharmaceutical sales representatives until 9:00am.

But just for this example let's say that you are able to work form 8am-5pm. Keep in mind that you are required to see 8-10 doctors a day Face-to-Face. And get their signatures for sample as well as make your 20-40 second sales presentation. Now if you can get more time with the doctor that's all well and good. But just in case you didn't know it these days doctors have become very, very busy. And you must keep in mind that Time Is Money! When the doctor is talking with a pharmaceutical representative he or she is not making any money.

Anyway , let's get back to our example of making the first call of the day. You have arrived at the doctor's office on time and there are already 3 other representatives waiting ahead of you to see the doctor. For our example let's say that each representative waits 30 minutes each before they are allowed back to see the doctor.

Now if that is the case you would have had to wait 1 hour and 30 minutes. As a result the time is already 10:30am before you ever get to see your first doctor for the day and you still have to wait another 30minutes in his office or in the sample closet before you actually see the doctor. Now it is already 11:00am or maybe later. You are just getting the opportunity to see the doctor. What this really means is you now only have 1hour or less left in the morning hours before 12:00 noon to see approximately 4-5 doctors before lunch time. If you don't see 4-5 doctors before lunch time you have to see even more doctors after lunch time because you are required to see a total of 8-10 doctors a day.

What this also means is if you encounter the same situation at your next office or if you have a long distance to drive before you get to the next office. You could very easily find yourself in a Very Stressful Situation. Each and every day that you go out to work. Because from all of my years of experience in this business you realistically need to see 4-5 doctors before 12:00 noon each day and another 4-5 doctors after lunch each day in order to achieve your required quota of daily doctor calls set for you by the company. So the big question is, What are you going to do if you find yourself in that situation? Another important question to ask yourself is, How would this make you feel each day if you had to work under these conditions every day?

But that's not all. As a part of the pharmaceutical sales representative's job they are required to make 1-2 retail pharmacy calls each day in addition to the regular 8-10 doctor office sales calls each day.

To make matter even more stressful the company along with the division manager has access a computer software program that enables them to analyze in great detail via vivid charts and graphs every single detail of a representative's daily activity at the push of a button. So even though a sales representative is working independently on their own from home and in the territory the powers to be are always watching the representative's every move on a daily basis. Some managers might tell you they are not but believe me they are. With this powerful software they can see on a screen what time you start your day, when you make your first call and each additional call, how much time you spend between before you make your next call, what area of your territory in which you make your calls, how many samples you leave, how many doctor signatures you get daily versus how many non signatures each day. Just so you will know the powers to be look down on your work if you have a high percentage of doctor call that do not have signatures with the call. The reason being the doctor's signature is confirmation to the company that the pharmaceutical representative has actually made a call on the doctor.

The reality of all this is even though you are working from home and you feel you are working independently controlling your day. You are not!! It all an Illusion!!! The fact of the matter is that from the time you start your day until the time you end you day. You are being monitored by someone from the company. Additionally because of all the electronic devices that are a part of the daily process you are forced to **Race With The Clock Everyday** in order to get all of the work done for the company. And I can tell you that Time Flies when you are racing from office to office and from city to city.

In contrast to the way the job was done in the earlier year s we had none of these obstacles to overcome and our time was use exactly the way we thought it should be used. Most of all we got the job done. Actually with the introduction of handheld electronic devices into pharmaceutical sales and the ability these devises have given the powers to be. Position of pharmaceutical sales has been changed forever. Or at least for as long as there is thing called pharmaceutical sales. Because just like many other jibs that have disappeared it is predicted that in the near future this career will no longer be available as we know it today. We will talk about that in a later chapter.

I think it is very, very important for you fully understand what is required to do this job so you will know what need to done.

Now lets take a look at the next variable **Geography**. What can I say? We have already talked a little about this one. What can I say? It's really very easy to figure this one out. Actually a good GPS devise will help you a lot with this one. Because with a good GPS you can simply put in your destination and it will tell you exactly how long it will take you to get there.

Last but not least. Let's take a look at **Availability.** This can be a very tricky one that can really mess up your call plans each day. Once you decide to accept a job as pharmaceutical sales representative and you begin calling on the doctors in your territory you will find that all doctors have specific days and times they are available to see pharmaceutical sales representatives. I hate to tell you this but they are not all the same. For example you could have 2 of your best doctors who are located at opposite end of the farthest points in your territory. Which could be at least 2 hours apart. As a result you will need to figure a way you schedule your time so that you can see these 2 doctors as well as your 100-150 others doctors 1-2 or more times with a 3-4 month period of time. What you will end up doing is having a varied mixture of days and different time schedules for all the doctors throughout your territory. As you have probably guessed it will be your responsibility to figure out a way to do this. Sometimes it is not possible. But one thing for sure the company doesn't care about any of your excuses about why you can't do it. All the care about is that you **Get The Job Done!**

Chapter 9

An Insider's View of How Contract Pharmaceutical Sales Works

To start this chapter off let's look at the typical interview process. As usual a candidate for a position in contract pharmaceutical sales interviews for an opening. For the most part the interview process is very much the same as it would be if you were interviewing for a job working for a traditional pharmaceutical company. One of the only differences is the process usually moves a lot faster because it seems the contract company is anxious to get a sales team in place because from the date the contract was signed with the client the money clock starts ticking. And as a result the contract pharmaceutical company is in a race again times to get the project up and running as fast as humanly possible. Why is this the case? Because the contract pharmaceutical company has made certain promises to the client or the manufacturer that it will achieve a certain number of total doctor call and generate a certain agreed upon total number of new prescription by certain predetermined times through the duration of the contract. Which is one of the reasons that some contracts end early because if the contract pharmaceutical company has not achieved a certain predetermined number of new prescription by a certain time. Depending on how much time is left on the contract there is no possible way that the new prescription goal will ever be reached. Therefore the client knows there in no reason to continue with the contract so they terminate the contract early.

So usually this agreed upon promise consists of the agreement that the field force the contract pharmaceutical company hires will make a specific number of doctor call by a specific date in time. Also the contract pharmaceutical company has agreed that the sale force will achieve a certain specific sales goal by a certain date in time.

And by doing so the contract pharmaceutical sales company will receive a financial bonus check of several hundred thousand dollars for achieving this goal. As well as if they don't achieve this financial goal the contract pharmaceutical company could possibly be charged a very large sum of money ranging in the hundreds of thousands of dollars by the client company. In addition to the periodic bonuses received by the Contract Pharmaceutical Sales Company if the Contract Pharmaceutical Sales Company achieves the long term new prescription goal established at the very beginning of the contract. The Contract Pharmaceutical Sales Company will receive a payment of several million dollars. Not to mention that at the very beginning of the contract the Contract Pharmaceutical Sales Company received and initial upfront payment of several million dollars to get the project started. Then out of this initial upfront payment the Contract Pharmaceutical Company sets it expense budget and salary budgets from which it will operate the overall project. That is one of the main reasons salaries in contract pharmaceutical sales are so much lower than when working for Big Pharma. The contract pharmaceutical sale company has a much smaller budget to work from so they feel they should keep expenses at a minimum it will much easier to turn a profit.

Which brings me to a discussion of some of those things the big pharmaceutical companies and major contract pharmaceutical companies don't want you to know about. I am confident that with this insider information you will be able to make much better decisions of how to function within this system. Without this information you will no doubt make many very costly mistakes.

You see from the very beginning of the interview the hiring manager is seeking to find the individual who he or she feels can do the best job. And at the much lower salary than traditionally offered for the job. So in contract pharmaceutical sales the job does not always go to the qualified individual. The job most often goes to the highest qualified candidate that is willing to take the lowest salary. The manager is striving to get the most he or she can get for the least amount of money. Keep in mind that the manager is working with a set predetermined budget for salaries. The manager is also looking for the individual who he or she feels will stay for the entire duration of the contract. You see once the contract starts the district manager does not want to have to look for, interview and hire a new person to bring onto an already active contract. Another reason this is the case is because a district manager many times is responsible for a very large territory and as a result is makes his job more difficult when he or she has to make special arrangements to go back into an area to hire a new person once the contract has already begun. Additional managers realize that if a person leaves a contract while the contract is already in force it could have a major negative impact on the Total Call Count Goal set forth in the contract agreement with the client.

Just imagine what would happen if a contract all of a sudden was to lose 1-2 people in different areas of the country at the same time. This would have a significant impact on the original call count goals and sales goal that contract company must achieve in order to receive the predetermined financial payout from the client. It could also mean that the contract company is not able to reach its sales goals and as a result experience a major financial. And if things get too bad the contract pharmaceutical company could stand to lose the entire contract.

Which could eventually translate into to the loss of millions of dollars in income to the contract pharmaceutical company. So as you can see the Contract Pharmaceutical Company and its field managers are under a tremendous amount of pressure to find and to keep their sales people on the job. They want to be sure to keep the sales people in the field working and running as fast as they can. Not mention that the contract pharmaceutical sales company also makes a percentage of all the salaries of all of the field sales force. Which adds up to millions of dollars.

Contract Pharmaceutical Sales Is Not The Job For Everyone

From my experience contract pharmaceutical sales is not the job for everyone. I think this is very important for an individual to understand before they get in this business. Or if you are already in this business it is a good thing to finally realize before you find yourself standing in the unemployment line with no place to turn for money to pay your bills.

I have found that if you are a person who is the head of the household. Or if you are a two income family and you depend on both incomes to survive. **Then pharmaceutical sales Is Not The Long Term Career Opportunity For You!!!!** Because if you are like most people who are married or single you depend on every dollar you make in order to pay your bills. But if you are going to work in pharmaceutical sales you have to change your mindset from what you have been taught up until now. In order to survive financially in this business you have to begin to depend less and less on the income you make from the job. Instead **You Must** shift your financial dependency solely from the job income to multiple sources of income. These days and on into the future you cannot depend on just the one income you earn from pharmaceutical sales. Because I can guarantee you that you will lose your income from pharmaceutical sales at different points in time should you decide to remain in this business. When this happens and if you are not prepared you will suffer financially as well as mentally.

On the other hand if you are in a situation where you are financially independent or your spouse/mate makes a very large income. And as a result the money you make from pharmaceutical sales is just all **Play Money for you to spend anyway you want.** Then pharmaceutical sales is **The Perfect Job for you!**

<u>Note</u>

Be aware that when you sign your employment contract with a contract pharmaceutical sales company you are agreeing to the fact that sometime in the future your job description is subject to change at the discretion of your employer. What this means is when the contract starts out you might have a job description that seems very enjoyable , reasonable and achievable. But as the contract progresses over time the employer has the right to change the job requirement of the job at will. As a result over time based on the sales success or lack of success of the entire contract entire contract. Your employer can begin to require that you begin working harder and longer than you initially agreed to do in order achieve the overall sales goal the company promised the client at the beginning of the contract. From my experience most contracts start out very mild with the normal sales requirement. Then based on the achieved goals of the sales team the job begins to get tougher and tougher just short of being almost unbearable. But what I have found is most people cannot just quit their job. So they stay and fight it out. What also happens about this time is you will see sales people starting to leave the contract in order to take new jobs elsewhere.

Here Is Something You Need To Know

Over the years before retiring from this business I had the opportunity to work directly for 7 of the world's largest pharmaceutical companies. I have also had the privilege to work for 3 of the largest contract pharmaceutical companies on at least 11 different projects. And as a result of working for that many companies I have had the opportunity to meet thousands of really nice people over the years. Simply because in contract pharmaceutical sales each time you start a new contract you are required to participate in a training program at a special training facility set up by the company. And as a result each time this occurs the contract company needs hundreds of new people to fill these positions for the contract. Due to that fact each time I would begin a new contract I would be in a position to meet and develop friendships with many different people from all over the United States. Many of these people I have kept up with and maintained friendships with. And as a result I have experienced first the pain many different people have gone through as result of the unexpected termination of a contract. As a result of working on over 11 different contracts what I have found to be the case it that even though the sales people sign on for a contract that has a duration of 1,2 3 or some specific length of time. You can expect a contract to end a few months early. Of the 11 or so contracts I have worked on there have been very few that have continued for the entire length of what said would be the duration of the contract. In many cases a long term contract actually on continues for only 6-8 months before it is canceled by the client. When working in contract pharmaceutical sales I have found that you must never forget that you are really a **Temporary Salesperson**. Its best to think of yourself as a **Temporary Sales** person and never start to think of yourself as a permanent sales person. And never let anything the corporate office tells you or your manager tells you make you begin to feel that you have any kind of job security. Because the truth is **You Have No Job Security.** And no matter how successful you are on one contract does not guarantee that you will be selected for another contract. Your ability to secure a new contract is only good for the contract you are currently on if you are lucky enough to secure one. One thing you must remember and understand. Even though a manager will tell you that if you do a good job on a particular contract you will be given special consideration for the next contract. That is not true because whenever a contract ends everyone is scrambling like rats in maze trying to find someone who can help them land a new contract. Even managers are thrown out into the cold with the sales representatives and are force to hit the street looking for a new contract jobs. As a result what you will find it that many people hop back and forth between different pharmaceutical companies like nomads in the desert.

Chapter 10

The End of Pharmaceutical Sales Is Near

This book would not be complete without me discussing several major events that are destined to have a major impact on the future of pharmaceutical sales as we know it today. The events I am referring to have been slowly, but surely creeping up on the industry for some time now. The powers to be and all the upper management of the pharmaceutical industry know these events are slowly changing the world of pharmaceutical sales. But they are quietly maintaining that everything is fine and anyone in pharmaceutical sales has nothing to be concerned about. When in reality they are shaking in their boots. But yet again the individual who is considering on beginning a career in pharmaceutical sales or the individual who is now in pharmaceutical sales will find themselves without a job as a result of the catastrophic events that are coming.

The events I am referring to will certainly and without a doubt change the face of pharmaceutical sales for centuries to come. To be more exact the events I am referring to are more like a series of major earthquakes that are centered with the pharmaceutical industry. And without a doubt these events could very easily wipe out the industry's massive revenues and reduce their empires to nothing more than crumpling rubble in the streets.

And this is a situation that has been slowly developing over a period of many years now. Big Pharma knows the end of an era of making massive profits is just around the corner and as a result they have begun to do a number of things to get ready for these devastating events that are coming. I have to tell you they are really desperate to keep this from happening so get ready because you will soon begin to see some major changes starting to take place.

Chapter 11

The Pharmaceutical Industry Is About To Change Forever!

Here is another situation the industry is being very, very quiet about. Several of the world's most profitable drugs are about to go off patent along with even more everyday drugs that we all know. I am talking about drugs like Viagra , Lipitor, Plavix, Advair and Seroquel just to name a few. Which means that as a result the pharmaceutical industry is going to **lose Billions of Dollars in obscene revenue** unless Big Pharma finds another way to Safe Guard and then Inject new life back into their profits machines. And they will. Simply by combining one drug with another and giving the 2 combined drugs a new name.

Yes that's right the pharmaceutical industry is about to go through a major paradigm shift that could end pharmaceutical sales as you know it today. Because the fact is Big Pharma is racing directly towards a **Patent Apocalypse** and as a result the pharmaceutical industry faces the loss of over 400 billion dollars in annual drug sales due to the sales of a tsunami of cheap generic drugs that will soon flood the market. What's even worse is we may see the results of this catastrophe very soon. When many blockbuster drug patents are scheduled to expire. You see ,what makes this situation so devastating is the majority of the pharmaceutical companies now have a product pipeline that is as dry as a bone sitting in the hot desert sun. As I said before this major catastrophe will all but destroy Big Pharma unless they begin buying up several smaller more innovative drug companies who have enough new blockbuster products that will automatically **Inject The Life** back into these crumbling financial giants that are surely on the brink of disappearing.

If you don't believe me just begin to watch the news everyday from now on and you will see for yourself that what I am saying is true. What does all of this mean to you? Well, if you are currently considering getting a job in pharmaceutical sales. Or if you are already in pharmaceutical sales. I am saddened to have to tell you this. **You Are Too Late! You have missed the boat!! The good old days are over!!!** The good old days when a pharmaceutical sales representative was a respected part of the medical community is gone. The days when pharmaceutical companies treated their field force like kings and queens are gone. The days when pharmaceutical sales was one of the highest paid careers are gone. The days when pharmaceutical sales was one of the most secure stable jobs in the marketplace are gone.

As a matter of fact the little bit of opportunity that still exists today is about to be stripped away too. And if you are already in pharmaceutical sales my recommendation to you is that you **Immediately Begin Developing Your Plan B Survival Strategy** because I can guarantee you that you will need it!

Now if you recall from the past chapters I identified a definite trend the pharmaceutical industry has followed since 1991 every time their profits have been threatened. Do you recall this trend? **They begin firing salespeople.**

So even if none of what I have said comes true. I have found that just the possibility of major financial loss causes the pharmaceutical industry to begin to **Plan for the Worse** in the event it happens. It only makes good business sense. And over a 30 year period of time I have found that since 1991the pharmaceutical industry has adopted a **Plan For The Worse Survival Business Strategy.** It has never failed yet just take a look back over the history of the industry since 1991 and you will clearly see this trend. And as I said another major shake up in coming.

But that's not all!! There is more. Even more devastating to pharmaceutical sales are the new Healthcare Reform Laws. Because as a result the entire healthcare industry will soon have to change the way things are done mainly because of the mandatory computerization of the doctor's office. As well as several other variables the result being that within the next 3-5 years pharmaceutical sales will no longer exists as it does today.

A good example of what I am saying is that for about 5 years or so now a few major pharmaceutical companies have been experimenting with a program they call eDetailing. The way this works is the doctor is given an incentive to go online and participate in an online detail sales presentation at the doctor's convenience. And for doing this the pharmaceutical company will give the doctor a certain reward for doing so. The doctor will also be given the option to order samples electronically at this time too. As a result the doctor is conditioned to engage in an interactive sales presentation at his or her convenience. The doctor gets a reward and the doctor can also order samples that will then be delivered directly to the doctor's office. Now which do you think a doctor would prefer to do considering the fact that doctors are now working harder to see more patients for less money? Think about it. After the Patent Apocalypse takes place, after all the mergers and buyouts, after Healthcare Reform Law is put into place and by time more lawsuits occur and they will. More and more pharmaceutical companies feel that eDetailing is a much safer more cost effective way to get their message across because by delivering their sales message this way the pharmaceutical company can control every part of the process from beginning to end. Resulting in less miscommunications by the sales representative and as a result far fewer lawsuits. Not to mention that by giving doctors the option to order samples online will save the pharmaceutical companies Billions of Dollars in expenses they now have.

Additionally from my research I have found that many doctors all over the United States are already receiving a variety of different kinds of different promotions in the mail from pharmaceutical companies that will allow the doctors to simply order the samples they need through the mail. Then the samples will be shipped directly to the doctor's office. **No pharmaceutical sales representative required.**

The point I am making is that in the very near future there will be far fewer if any pharmaceutical sales representatives and the few who will remain will be made up of individuals that have some kind of formal medical educational training. Yes very soon you will see these changes starting to take place. I sincerely hope that you will take begin right away preparing yourself for the job you will begin doing while you have time before the major changes begin to take place. Don't wait because if you lose your job and you are not prepared financially you could very easily lose home your car and even worse your family. Good Luck.

Your Potential Job Opportunities After Your Pharmaceutical Sales Job Is Over

It would seem that after working as highly trained pharmaceutical sales representative for 5,10, 15 20 years or more. Companies everywhere would be jumping over backwards to hire you. After all for all those years while you worked as a pharmaceutical sales representative you were managing a territory that was worth millions of dollars to the pharmaceutical company. And as a pharmaceutical sales representative who was in charge of that territory you were first required to study very complex pharmaceutical products and learn all about them at a level which enabled you to speak to doctors , nurses and other medical professional on the same level as if you had gone to medical school your self. You were also given the responsibility to figure out who the best customers were out of hundreds of doctors within your territory. You were responsible for developing productive relationships with those people. You were responsible for servicing those people by educating them, supporting them as well as convincing them to buy lots more of your product. Not to mention providing them with millions of dollars in samples each month based on the strict governmental rules and regulations that I mentioned earlier.

In addition to those responsibilities you were required to maintain a computer database of all those customers daily by inputting critical information about those customers and your interactions with those customers as well as the sample accountability and other territory information each day. My friend I am sure that I don't have to remind you. That's alot of responsibility and as a result you earned every penny of the money you made while working as a pharmaceutical sales representative. So it would seem that with so much solid , real world experience finding another high paying professional job once you left pharmaceutical sales would be as easy as can be. Well I am sorry to say it is not. Because for some reason most other employers outside of the pharmaceutical industry have very little respect for the training and the work that pharmaceutical sales representatives have acquired. As a result what you will find is a cold cruel job market out there waiting on you that has very, very little respect and recognition of all the hard work that you put in while you were working a pharmaceutical sales representative. So don't be surprised when you put your resume on ZipRecruiter.com, Indeed.com , Monster.com, CareerBuilder.com or any of the other job website. The majority of companies that greet you with open arms will be all of the low paying, low skilled , low level employers who are just looking for warm bodies to throw on the wall to see who sticks for a few weeks. Like Uber, Lyft , CPI Security, ADT security several different insurance companies, local publications in need of sales people to sell ad space, local roofing companies , other local home service related companies and many others like them. As well as host of MLM and Network marketing companies and other companies trying to sell you on spending money for a business opportunity. And those same companies will continue to contact you week after week, month after month hoping that sooner or later you will get desperate enough to go to work for them.

My best advice to you is to go back to school right away and get a certification in some career opportunity that is predicted to be one of the Hot Career Opportunities of the day and the Future!!! Do not wait around thinking that another Big Executive Job like pharmaceutical sales is going to drop in your lap. Because it Will Not Happen. You will not be offered another high level executive sales job on the same level as the job you had as a pharmaceutical sales rep without some advanced training certification training.

Resources

If you would like to uncover more information on this subject simply do a keyword search using the following keyword phrases:

Keyword Research

The end of pharmaceutical sales
Is pharmaceutical sales dead
The phase out of pharmaceutical sales
The future of pharmaceutical sales

Additional Resources

Must Read!!!!

http://www.cafepharma.com/boards/threads/i-had-the-balls-to-leave-pharma.619058/page-9

http://www.cafepharma.com/boards/threads/i-had-the-balls-to-leave-pharma.619058/page-8

http://www.cafepharma.com/boards/threads/i-had-the-balls-to-leave-pharma.619058/page-7

http://www.cafepharma.com/boards/threads/i-had-the-balls-to-leave-pharma.619058/page-6

http://www.cafepharma.com/boards/threads/i-had-the-balls-to-leave-pharma.619058/page-2

http://www.cafepharma.com/boards/threads/careers-after-pharma-real-success-stories-please.480167

1. The Prescription Drug Marketing Act
2. Healthcare Reform Bill
3. Pharmaceutical sales layoff stats
4. **eDetailing The Future of Pharmaceutical Sales-The** http://www.tapanray.in/e-detailing-the-future-of-pharmaceutical-sales/

5. **Money , Math and Medicine** (Great article on how contract pharmaceutical sales works)

http://www.forbes.com/forbes/2010/1122/private-companies-10-quintiles-dennis-gillings-money-medicine_2.html

These are just a few of the many resources that await you in cyberspace if you just take the time to look for them. I have found that the answers to many of your questions are available to you online. Also if you are going to remain in pharmaceutical sales or if you are interested in getting a job in pharmaceutical sales you must develop the mindset that you are going to continue to learn everything you can about what is going on in the industry each and every day. So you will always know what direction the industry is going. If nothing else always research and investigate the company you are working for so that you will know well in advance of any major changes that are about to occur. Just remember these 2 indicators. If your company just bought another company or if your company has just been bought by another company. Some major changes in the sales force are about to occur to both.

Closing Remarks

Please read this very carefully. Even though pharmaceutical sales is going through many changes. And the career opportunity is not what it used to be. There will still be some opportunities available for only a select few people, given all the uncertainty and lack of job stability that will remain in this industry. If you feel that you are the kind of person that has the courage and skills that will be required. I encourage you to go ahead and give it a try. But the one thing I would recommend is that you not develop a total dependence on the income you will make as a result of doing the job. Because I believe the industry will remain unstable and very volatile for many years to come. As a result your job income could be taken away from you at anytime. So always maintain a **Plan B Survival Strategy** at all times. And don't wait until you need it to start developing it. Be proactive. Begin developing your **Plan B Survival Strategy** while you still have a job.